Power and Vulnerability

Reflections on Mark 9

Roland Riem

Anglican Chaplain, University of Nottingham

GROVE BOOKS LIMITED
BRAMCOTE NOTTINGHAM NG9 3DS

Contents

The two chapters of this book approach the story of Jesus healing the epileptic demoniac (Mark Chapter 9.14-29) from two different and complementary directions. The first sets out to discover where power can be found in situations in which we seem powerless and vulnerable. We find it in the power to offer ourselves in all our vulnerability to God. This is true prayer, which we hear expressed in the cry, 'I believe; help my unbelief!' The second chapter wonders how the power we do have can serve those we meet who are oppressed and who suffer. We find that if power is used with vulnerability, to enter into the suffering of another, then we can be agents of God's deliverance from evil. This is true authority, which we see exercised in the healing ministry of Jesus.

Acknowledgements

I would like to thank the Association of Christian Psychiatrists for first giving me the opportunity to formulate these thoughts for their annual conference. Thanks, too, to the Revds Graham Piggott and Russ Parker, and to Susanne Thompson of Grove Books, who all helped in the revision of the manuscript.

The Cover Illustration is by Sophie Hacker

First Impression October1994
ISSN 0262-799X
ISBN 1 85174 280 8

1
The Power of Vulnerability

The Problem of Accepting Vulnerability

Whatever we might read about vulnerability, and however much we might admire others who seem not to have grown too many skins of cynicism or caution, few of us find it easy to be vulnerable. It is not easy to be open to hurt, disappointment, rejection or abuse—and this is the danger of vulnerability. It's a condition that most of us, most of the time, prefer to avoid. The temptation is always to try to hide away from the pain, to shut ourselves off or to shut others out. The words of a famous song by Paul Simon describe a common strategy for self-preservation:

> 'I have my books and my poetry to protect me;
> I am shielded in my armour,
> Hiding in my room,
> Safe within my womb.
> I touch no one and no one touches me.
> I am a rock, I am an island.
> And a rock feels no pain.
> And an island never cries.'

All of us have to some extent learned to survive like this. We avoid the risk of openness. We need our defences to deal with people, and, if we are honest, we need them to deal with God too. Our heavenly Father is sometimes the last person we want to face.

But to be human is to be vulnerable. Shutting ourselves off and shutting others out is a long-term recipe for despair and isolation. It is impossible truly to love anything without running the risk of being hurt. So in life we are often caught between our instincts to play safe and our desire for a greater wholeness for all that we love. That is why we instinctively respond to the story in Chapter 9 of Mark's Gospel which tells of a despairing father who comes to Jesus to see whether he can do something to save his son from the clutches of destruction. Jesus stirs him to the cry of faith, 'I believe; help my unbelief'. Whatever else it may be saying, this plea rings out with pain and honesty from a bleeding heart, from someone who is reaching out with empty hands in an outburst of agonised hope.

We feel most vulnerable when we are powerless. Being powerless is worse than being weak. Weakness need not cut us off from seeing a way through the present, but powerlessness leaves us unable to do what we want or to have what we want. And the more we want something, the more we have tried to have it and failed in our attempts, the more powerless and the more vulnerable we feel. Then the temptation is greatest to turn away from God; and the story in Mark's Gospel becomes important, because it teaches that God's will can be done even when everything around us seems dark, and even when God himself seems to be plunging our hearts into darkness. God waits on us to let our defences down, letting him see our emptiness and fear, and in that poverty of spirit to offer our real trust that he can do something beyond expectation and imagination.

Exploring the Passage: Mark 9.14-29

Mark's Gospel is the darkest, the most tense and concentrated, and the most dramatic of Gospels. Everything in Mark happens 'at once' or 'immediately', depending on your translation! You will probably notice as you read the passage that powerlessness and the vulnerability resulting from it is a major theme: the disciples can't heal the boy, so they lay themselves open to attack from the scribes; the scribes protect themselves from showing their own powerlessness by arguing instead of attempting an exorcism; the boy's father is on the verge of despair—he has tried everything and failed; and the boy himself is hardly a subject at all, more an object argued over by men and attacked by a malicious 'spirit of dumbness'. We shall look at this story to see how vulnerability needn't lead to despair but can be the gate through which God comes to save us.

PLEASE READ THE PASSAGE NOW IN YOUR OWN BIBLE

Jesus, Peter, James and John have come down from the mountain of Transfiguration. No sooner has that scene ended, than they walk into conflict:

And when they came to the disciples, they saw a great crowd about them, and scribes arguing with them.

It is a sterile argument, about authority. In those days the possibility of exorcism was not in question; the issue was, who was allowed to do it. The scribes and disciples were locked in argument, getting nowhere about whether disciples had the right to do what they had done, or rather had failed to do.

And immediately all the crowd, when they saw him, were greatly amazed, and ran up to him and greeted him.

What a dramatic contrast between the sterility of argument and the authority of Jesus! He brings freshness to scene. There is a sudden astonishment, an eagerness to see him, which draws our attention to Jesus and away from the problems of the disciples and scribes. The stage is set to learn a general lesson of faith from the Teacher, quite apart from the bickering which has preceded it.

> *And he asked them, 'What are you discussing with them?' And one of the crowd answered him, 'Teacher, I brought my son to you, for he has a dumb spirit; and where it seizes him, it dashes him down; and he foams and grinds his teeth and becomes rigid; and I asked your disciples to cast it out and they were not able.'*

Jesus draws the crowd into dialogue with a question. The adult who has most at stake in this episode answers for them all, spilling out his catalogue of woes. Recognising Jesus' authority, he calls him 'Teacher'. It was Jesus whom he had been trying to seek out, not his disciples. Now he tells the Teacher both the chronic and the immediate problem. The boy's chronic problem we would call epilepsy (though it's more than that, as we shall see); the immediate problem is that he is helpless—so is the father, and so are the disciples. We feel sympathy for the man. We appreciate his problem, and we sympathise with the disciples, too, with their inability to do anything about it. So Jesus words come as a shock:

> *And he answered them, 'O faithless generation, how long am I to be with you? How long am I to bear with you?'*

This faithless generation includes both the crowd and the disciples. We will return to the man soon, for now we will think about the disciples. Surely the disciples had had faith? They had tried to exorcise the demon; they were confident of success, but they failed. And yet Jesus takes their failure as sign of faithlessness. How is this possible?

The answer lies in the disciples' self-reliance. We can look back in the Gospel and find three ways in which they might have grown overconfident. First, they have the power of a *successful role model*. In Mk 1.34 we read about Jesus that 'he healed many who were sick with various diseases, and cast out many demons; and he would not permit the demons to speak, because they knew him'. Secondly, they have the power of a *command*. In Mk 6.7 Jesus called in to him the twelve…and gave them authority over unclean spirits. Lastly, the disciples had experienced the power of *previous success*. Mk 6.13 says 'so they went out…and they cast out many demons, and anointed with oil many that were sick and healed them'. When they were relying on God this was what could happen.

The disciples are included among the faithless generation because they presume upon their faith, which turns out here to be more a matter of self-confidence. But the disciples are going to be taught by Jesus, through the way he deals with the boy and with the faithlessness of the boy's father. So Jesus commands:

> *'Bring him to me.' And they brought the boy to him; and when the spirit saw him immediately it convulsed the boy, and he fell on the ground and rolled about, foaming at the mouth.*

The spirit recognises the power of Jesus and throws down the gauntlet. The boy is completely possessed and powerless.

> *And Jesus asked his father, 'How long has he been like this.' And he said, 'From childhood. And it has often cast him into the fire and into the water, to destroy him; but if you can do anything, have pity on us and help us.'*

Jesus isn't making a medical diagnosis by asking politely, as doctors are supposed to, 'Now what seems to be the problem?' The problem has already manifested itself! Once again, a question is asked to draw a response. This time Jesus is more personal and direct. His challenge provokes a more personal response and a despairing plea from the father for some sort of help. The father never doubts Jesus' compassion, but his hope has been choked by the malicious spirit whose power is crushing not just the boy but his whole family. 'Have mercy on us (all)', he pleads.

The father does not dare hope for deliverance. He will settle for some token of compassion, however small and mean. Once again this is faithlessness. We know what sort of faith Jesus can work with because we read the story of the healing of the leper in Chapter 1 of Mark's Gospel: 'And a leper came to him beseeching him, and kneeling said to him "If you will you can make me clean". Moved with pity he stretched out his hand and touched him, and said to him, "I will; be clean". And immediately the leprosy left him, and he was made clean' (1.40-42).

> *And Jesus said to him, '"If you can!" All things are possible to him who believes.'*

Jesus turns the father's words round and rejoins: not if I can, but if you can; you can if you believe. We are reminded of that great promise in Matthew's Gospel, 'Whatever you ask in prayer, you will receive if you have faith' (21.22). Jesus' words point out the lack of faith in this episode so far; but in the same rebuke there is also a promise that despair need not have the final word. Jesus' words provoke a response of faith, which the man now gives:

> *Immediately the father of the child cried out and said, 'I believe; help my unbelief!'*

Immediately! This is where human faith springs up and the power of God can be brought into situation. It is certainly not the self-reliance of disciples. So what sort of faith is it?

The Vulnerability of Faith

The great Reformed theologian John Calvin, noticing the apparent contradiction between the father's profession of belief and unbelief, claimed it to be a common experience of all Christians: 'As our *faith* is never perfect, it follows that we are partly *unbelievers*; but God forgives us, and exercises such forbearance towards us, as to reckon us believers on account of a small portion of faith.'

But if God does have to forgive this kind of faith we do not find evidence of it in the story; rather, it is exactly what seems to let the power of God into the situation. God doesn't have to make up or overlook some lack in how much we believe before he can act for us. Healing follows on immediately from the father's cry, and Jesus' concern is not that the man's faith is insufficient, but that a crowd is gathering who might misinterpret what he is about to do.

The story is telling us that in one respect the father's faith is perfect. His words are a perfect example of sincere trust in, and eager desire for, a hidden God. This cry from the depths is the sort God can and does use, as Mark will suggest even more dramatically in Chapter 15, where Jesus' cry from the cross, 'My God, my God, why hast thou forsaken me?' is met by the centurion's confession, 'Truly this man was the Son of God.' The father's cry is not lacking in faith. It is both a confession of trust in a hidden God and a confession of human helplessness before God provoked by Christ's word. Faith's object has become nothing less than God. He it is who has become the hidden focus in the exchange between the father and the Lord, and this is the vital, practical lesson for the boy's father and all Christ's disciples: seeing ourselves as we truly are we see unbelief; looking to God as he truly is we believe. But the same faith underlies *both* responses, and this faith is the door through which God can come in power.

Faith is not the same as (self-)confidence before God. We have already seen that in the story. Faith hasn't made the father *feel* powerful where before he felt powerless. He remains vulnerable, unable to save himself; the difference now is that all that he is and all that he lacks is offered to God through Jesus. Faith is openness, not self-concern dressed up in religious language. As Eduard Schweizer puts it, faith is 'unconditional receptiveness' to the action of God. It's about letting oneself be vulnerable to God, about looking up from the painful conditions that are making us want to shut ourselves off and others out. The lesson is that for those who truly trust God, to the extent that they stop hiding behind their powerlessness, God's power knows no limits.

I have spelled out this point of Mark's story very briefly. Now we have to catch up on discovering that it might be true for us. Perhaps we too can make the journey from helplessness to receptiveness and learn how this vulnerability brings with it new possibilities of spiritual power.

A Parable of Vulnerability

One of the best illustrations of how helpless Christians can become in the face of despair comes from the fourteenth century, from the 51st Chapter of Mother Julian's *Revelations of Divine Love*, usually called the parable of the lord and the servant. There are two main themes in it. The first recalls the fall of Adam (though with no element of wilful disobedience in it) and the second recalls the fall of the incarnation, as Christ enters the vale of suffering. Mother Julian shares these visions partly to encourage those who feel bogged down in faith.

'I saw two persons in bodily likeness, that is to say a lord and a servant; and with that God gave me spiritual understanding. The lord sits in state, in rest and in peace. The servant stands before his lord, respectfully, ready to do his lord's will. The lord looks on his servant very lovingly and sweetly and mildly. He sends him to a certain place to do his will. Not only does the servant go, but he dashes off and runs at great speed, loving to do his lord's will. And soon he falls into a dell and is greatly injured; and then he groans and moans and tosses about and writhes, but he cannot rise or help himself in any way. And of all this, the greatest hurt which I saw him in was lack of consolation, for he could not turn his face to look on his loving lord, who was very close to him, in whom is all consolation; but like a man who was for the time extremely feeble and foolish, he paid heed to his feelings and his continuing distress, in which distress he suffered seven great pains. The first was the severe bruising which he took in his fall, which gave him great pain. The second was the clumsiness of his body. The third was the weakness which followed these two. The fourth was that he was blinded in his reason and perplexed in his mind, so much so that he had almost forgotten his own love. The fifth was that he could not rise. The sixth was the pain most astonishing to me, and that was that he lay alone. I looked all around and searched, and far and near, high and low, I saw no help for him. The seventh was that the place in which he lay was narrow and comfortless and distressful.'

Julian gives her reader a list of effects of the unfortunate servant's fall into the ditch. There in her vulnerability she feels physical pain, embarrassment, a sense of impotence, anxiety, a sense of being trapped and isolated; but the sixth result, we read, comes as a surprise. This is a sense of alienation, an awareness that she is in some sense outcast. We can imagine that this is the father's feeling in Mark's story as he and his boy sit outside the argument between the disciples and the scribes, and that this is the feeling behind the words, 'have pity on us.' The stigma of possession has cast the whole family adrift from society.

So Julian helps us remember that vulnerability is not nice or presentable. There are many reasons to lose faith and hope when you have fallen and are trapped and alone and unable to help yourself. And this state is far more painful than those situations where you choose to be vulnerable and can see ways to exploit your vulnerability. For example, I chose to be a University Chaplain who works as a guest within an academic institution. My job does not fit into the recognised categories, being neither academic nor academic-related nor welfare nor support. But this gives chaplains power to do things that others cannot, like drawing people together within the academic community, encouraging students to explore and discover faith, and noticing patterns of common concern across departments. We are fortunate that our role (in our university at least) is recognised, valued and welcomed by many, and that usually makes up for the feeling of working on the margins.

Being stuck in a ditch is much more wounding than choosing to be confined to the edge of a field. Julian's parable is for the fallen because it says to those who are seeking God but who have lost hope in him that God is ready to take pity on them and to rescue them:

> 'Then this courteous lord said this: See my beloved servant, what harm and injuries he has had and accepted in my service for my love, yes, and for his good will. Is it not reasonable that I should reward him for his fright and his fear, his hurt and all his woe?...Otherwise, it seems to me that I should be ungracious.'

Dark Dimensions of Vulnerability

Julian's parable has been useful to remind us how painful vulnerability can be and also to see that there is rescue in God. Her parable is particularly apt for Christians wearied and wounded in God's service. But the story Mark tells can offer Christians even more courage than Julian's, for it gives us an example of the overcoming of an extreme vulnerability, caused by dark dehumanising and oppressive forces. We read in Mark that a spirit of dumbness has brought a father and his boy to seek Jesus' mercy. Though the symptoms roughly correspond to those of epilepsy, and we see the boy healed and 'up on his own two feet' in the end, we have to notice that the boy is cured by a malicious spirit coming out of him at Jesus' command. The full story is one of conflict with, and deliverance from, destructive powers.

How we understand this passage depends on the assumptions we bring to it. The New Testament world is familiar with demons, led by Satan, and of spirits of various sorts, good, neutral, or bad. The bad ones were thought responsible for causing disease and infirmity. Some now argue that people believed in demon-sickness because they did not know the natural cause of certain diseases but reasoned that they must have some cause. So they put sickness down to the supernatural world of demons and spirits. Thus we should not take exorcism stories at face value but see them as healings that have been dramatised to show Jesus' authority over the evil that people suffer when they fall sick.

Others want to see demons as standing for something more than the evil of sickness. They notice that demons are depicted as destructive power and that in the western world medical understanding has, until recently, seen disease as a malfunction of an individual body. Even the recent emphasis on psychosomatic (mind-body) disorders misses out on recognising the effects of social and political forces on human destiny. So, they argue, demons are more than out-dated language for healing, they are a way of talking about wider, objective forces outside the body that oppress us.

Few would deny the power of social, economic and political forces to oppress us. It is also important not to privatise the act of deliverance; Jesus does far more in this story than save a soul from an evil spirit. On the other hand, it shouldn't be assumed that the world is so simple that explanations from medical or social science of human disease and misfortune provide a complete explanation. A spiritual interpretation of events has its own integrity. It is not just another language to use to give natural causes a divine meaning. Sometimes it may offer the most fundamental account of events. The writers of the New Testament were aware of the natural realm, but didn't feel bound always to explain things in natural terms.

We can make the point about finding a basic explanation more clearly by comparing it to the different levels you would find in that popular genre, the Western; the main reason the baddies get their come-uppance is not because they bungle the robbery (the economic reason), nor because they get shot (the medical!), but precisely because they are baddies (the moral). It is their badness that really causes their downfall, and the economic and medical explanations turn out to be more like answers to 'how' questions rather than to the basic question of 'why.'

Christians believe in a God who works in and through all the forces of creation, but also in One who exists apart from creation. God is Spirit, whose purposes can be seen at work in the world. Our belief in this sort of God allows us to see God's hand at work in the 'natural' world which is often described in scientific terms; and it can also prevent us from ruling out the possibility of a distinct spiritual dimension behind and beyond our material world, which might include both good and evil.

There are three reasons why we should go on to acknowledge a distinct realm of spiritual evil. First, because the gospels give a careful and quite precise demonology. Satan is seen as an active agent opposing God who sometimes acts independently (Mk 1.13), sometimes through his agents, the demons (Mk 1.23), and sometimes through people. For example, when Peter tries to deter Jesus from setting out on the road to suffering, rejection and death Jesus says to him, 'Get behind me, Satan.' Secondly, it makes sense of our own experience of the world: however much political and social analysis is made on the media about the mindless and irrational slaughter in the Balkans, for example, it never captures the active, wilful destructiveness of evil behind it. Thirdly, we still hear accounts of evil attacking individual lives, especially in stories of deliverance from those parts of the church which have not been so trapped by rational and scientific explanations.

Like Jesus, we've spent time asking questions of this situation to see the *root* cause of vulnerability in this case. Paying attention to particulars will help us to know what is happening in the story. And it's easy to draw the wrong lessons. Those who say that what the Bible describes as 'demonisation' is nothing but a medical condition are going seriously to mislead themselves. Jesus doesn't simply bring healing in this story; he brings deliverance to the heart of this family's problem with a sign of resurrection:

And when Jesus saw that a crowd came running together, he rebuked the unclean spirit saying to it, 'You dumb and deaf spirit, I command you, come out of him, and never enter him again.' And after crying out and convulsing him terribly, it came out, and the boy was like a corpse; so that most of them said, 'He is dead.' But Jesus took him by the hand and lifted him up, and he arose.

The boy's recovery is not just a healing but a sign of resurrection. The boy has been a battle ground on which a superhuman drama has been played out. Throughout he has been passive, a victim. He has not had epilepsy; it— this spirit—has had him. That is why the New Jerusalem Bible is right to entitle this section 'The Epileptic Demoniac'. We are not just dealing here with a medical problem. Only at the end of the story when the boy arises does he become an active subject, a person in his own right.

Prayer—the Hidden Power of Vulnerability

The lesson of faith here is that God can bring his power to bear on people in situations of wilful destructiveness. It is evil that Jesus removes by prayer, directly, by casting out the spirit attacking the boy, and not just indirectly by removing the stigma of possession from the whole family. So Christians who care for those with chronic illnesses such as dementia and epilepsy may not find their trusting cry of faith and sincere desire for God met with physical healing; but the prayer offered out of their vulnerability will call down God's power over evil, and cast out its effects. In other words, prayer will always have a personal and spiritual effect for good but may not always bring about a improvement in material health.

It would be a mistake, then, to claim this story as a guarantee that the right sort of prayer will get people what they most want. The story isn't an invitation to use faith to manipulate God; it is a much darker, less ego-centred drama than that. We are taken into a cosmic struggle in which we find everyone but Jesus helpless and no one sure what is possible but Jesus. The seeds of deliverance are sown in Mark's story as the crowd are encouraged by Jesus to give over their powerlessness and faithlessness to him. The seeds are watered as his word causes further pain in the boy and heart-searching in the father. They germinate when the pain and probing provoke faith in God through Jesus Christ. But the tension in the story is never completely resolved: will the disciples learn this lesson of faith?

> *And when Jesus had entered the house, his disciples asked him privately, 'Why could we not cast it out?' And he said to them, 'This kind cannot be driven out by anything but prayer.'*

This prayer is not like staking a claim on the impossible. The leper whom Jesus heals in Chapter 1 of Mark's Gospel pleads, *'If you will* you can make me clean.' He is certain of what he wants and he prevails upon Jesus to hear him, but he certainly doesn't presume upon him. Neither is the prayer of faith about latching on to a hoped-for outcome like a dog with a bone.[1] The father of the demoniac epileptic never claims deliverance for his son as a right. He is not even clear as he cries out about what God might do; rather, he stops hiding the helplessness that caused him to expect so little of Jesus and lets go of it along with the hope that brought him looking for Jesus. His unbelief and his belief spring from pain in an act of naked trust. It's this trust and desire, forged from the raw materials of human darkness and despair, that has spiritual power, because it calls down from a compassionate God deliverance from evil.

Equally, it would be mistaken to turn this pattern into a universal spiritual law, because in the end it's neither the vulnerability nor the prayer that is powerful in itself but only the God who cares about our suffering and hears our prayer. This is implied in the father's cry which ends with the admission of lack. His faith is not complete by itself but opens out onto God.

---

1 Mark 11.24 does not mean this either. It presupposes that what a disciple asks for in prayer will leave God free to give whatever he wills in response to faith.

It is the exact opposite of the self-reliance denounced by Jesus as faithlessness. Nevertheless, it seems true that vulnerability laid before the throne of God in prayer is a powerful weapon in the battle against evil. Julian of Norwich was clearly hoping to elicit this sort of trusting response from her discouraged readers by telling her parable of a lord ready to rescue his fallen servant. So too was another spiritual writer of her age, the anonymous author of a manual on contemplative prayer, *The Cloud of Unknowing*. He gives this advice to those whose prayer was hampered by 'sinful thoughts and impulses':

> When you feel that you can in no way put down these thoughts, cower down under them like a poor wretch and a coward overcome in battle, and reckon it to be a waste of time for you to strive any longer against them. In this way, though you are in the hands of your enemies, you give yourself up to God... This humility merits God himself coming down in his power to avenge you against your enemies, to take you up, to cherish you and to dry your spiritual eyes...

Putting ourselves and others into God's hands is difficult, sometimes seemingly impossible, when we are vulnerable. How can I put myself, my family or friends into God's hands when it is his hands which are crushing us and providing no means of escape? The temptation is to hold back our desire for change altogether, or to offer what we think he expects or requires. At those moments it is worth remembering that vulnerability has a dark side, that God is not the monster of our imagination. Rather, his hands are open and aching, waiting to be drawn into the battle against evil by prayer. The stuff we most want to hold back from God—our trust, our anger, our hurt, our unbelief—is exactly what God most needs from us, because this is the stuff of our real selves, which amazingly God has chosen to wait upon before he acts to save us. Our vulnerability only becomes powerful when we let God get hold of it.

2
The Vulnerability of Power

The Problem of Power

The story of the epileptic demoniac in Mark Chapter 9 has shown us the power that vulnerability can have through prayer. The character who has taught us this lesson is the father of the boy. He does the only fruitful thing anyone can do when one is powerless. But there is another character in the story who can also teach a lesson of faith, and he is the Lord himself. Mark believes that Jesus Christ is the Son of God (that means, at the very least, in a unique relationship to God), but this does not stop him painting a portrait of Jesus as one who stands with his fellow creatures, teaching them in person what it means to be faithful. So the way Jesus uses his power to deliver the powerless is an example to us of how we are to learn to use our own gifts, skills and graces to the benefit of our neighbour.

Anglican Christians, the ones I know best, are often rather embarrassed by power. They may call God 'Almighty' in prayer and ask him to send them out in the power of the Holy Spirit at the end of a service of Holy Communion, but afterwards they tend to quickly revert to the language of kindness, service and love. Perhaps this is in part because few of us feel ourselves to be powerful. Partly this may be because we confuse power and control. A preacher who cannot manipulate his congregation to do what he wants might deny that he has any power, not realising that he can very effectively induce anger and guilt among his hearers. Children are much more aware of what they can achieve by hectoring!

It is also true that even powerful people live under heavy constraint of circumstance. This is an irony in an age that talks so much about the value of freedom of choice. In my university, I visited one of the most respected and eminent professors, the inventor of a revolutionary medical technique. More and more he found himself the victim of his own success. He had less and less time for research. The only way out for him would be early retirement, and of course that would never be offered to him. Other lecturers, wanting to advance their own careers and needing to conform with the latest educational decree, hop through one professional hoop after the next, leaving little time for their families, recreation or even eating. Often sandwiches have to be grabbed in the office. And some are as lonely as they are busy. The demand for efficiency and economy presses in on everyone. We seem hemmed in by the natural laws of economics and the pressures of the demands of society.

As well as being unaware of their power, though, Christians may simply be embarrassed to admit to the power they have over others. There is a variation on an old saying that goes, 'Power corrupts; absolute power is even nicer!' It makes the point that power is open to misuse and can be corrupting. Power lays us open to temptation; having it makes us morally vulnerable. Some of the religious leaders of Jesus' day had been corrupted by power. Each gospel has a slightly different view of them.[2] In Mark the leaders are frequently wrong, because, as Jesus tells them plainly, they 'know neither the scriptures nor the power of God' (12.24). They define the Law as a set of legalistic prescriptions not, as Jesus does, in terms of exercising love (12.28-31). They do not know the power of God either, as they attribute Jesus' exorcism to the power of the devil (3.22). Their judgement is flawed because they fear what others will think of them (11.32, 12.12). They base what they do on the power they can command among the people. Their authority does not come from God.

Because we do have power and often seek it and use it with little aware-ness, Christians have a responsibility to acknowledge the power they have. Power is a gift from a mighty God, and like all gifts power needs to be used well. Jesus had unique spiritual power and authority, but he used it to enter into the suffering and sin of his fellow human beings. He showed his power in vulnerability. The 'vulnerability of power', then, needn't only mean that quality of power which makes it morally dangerous; it can also stand for power's supreme fulfilment, as we see it exercised in the life of Jesus Christ.

Jesus' Authority—the Vulnerability of Power

In contrast to the religious leaders, Jesus derives his authority from God, as the transfiguration scene before the exorcism in Chapter 9 has stressed in one dark and mysterious moment:

> And a cloud overshadowed them, and a voice came out of the cloud, 'This is my beloved Son; listen to him.' And suddenly looking around they no longer saw anyone with them but Jesus only.

Jesus stands alone, but for one moment the disciples have seen and heard what empowers him, a relationship with God his Father. In John's gospel Jesus' sonship is spelled out far more explicitly, but Mark presents Jesus' use of power is a sign of his identity, which at the beginning of the gospel only the demons recognise. They are silenced by Jesus because they distort the truth of his identity. There is a terrible danger that the Messiah's mission may be understood. He is not someone who brings an easy deliverance to his people; he is the suffering servant who has come to lay down his life as a ransom for many. When Peter rebukes Jesus for teaching this, he is in turn

---

2   Mark Powell, *What is Narrative Criticism?* (SPCK, London 1990) pp 60f.

rebuked with the astonishing words 'Get behind me Satan! For you are not on the side of God, but of men.' Then in Mark 8.34-7 Jesus sets before the people, as well as his disciples, the difficult way for each of them to follow:

'If any man would come after me, let him deny himself and take up his cross and follow me. For whoever would save his life will lose it; and whoever loses his life for my sake and the gospel's will save it. For what does it profit a man, to gain the whole world and forfeit his life?'

Unlike Luke, Mark does not often draw attention to Jesus' prayer-relationship with God. But clearly being alone with God is crucial to his whole mission. Mark makes this point in the programmatic statement in Chapter 1.35-39. He is clear that Jesus speaks and acts with God's authority and that prayer lies at the heart of his ministry.

And in the morning, a great while before day, he rose and went out to a lonely place, and there he prayed. And Simon and those who were with him pursued him, and they found him and said to him, 'Everyone is searching for you.' And he said to them, 'Let us go on to the next towns, that I may preach there also; for that is why I came out. And he went throughout all Galilee, preaching in their synagogues and casting out demons.

This means that a link can be made between the story in Chapter 9 of the casting out of the spirit of dumbness and the character of Christ's mission. The story need not be taken too narrowly as a lesson that prayer gives Jesus the power to deliver. The whole picture is much more interesting than that, because it's not just the boy who is healed but his father; and the two healings take the Lord deeper into suffering service.

Two verses before the incident Jesus is once again warning the disciples:

'How is it written of the Son of Man, that he should suffer many things and be treated with contempt?'

Jesus then walks into a conflict in which he involves himself, which he soon discovers, results from the faithlessness of his disciples and the ignorance of the crowd. Like the prophets who had gone before him, he has to stand with sorrow against God's people to proclaim God's judgement. The best known example of this come after God speaks to Elijah in a still small voice, when Elijah complains 'the people of Israel have forsaken thy covenant, thrown down thy altars, and slain thy prophets with the sword; and I, only I, am left, and they seek my life, to take it away.' We find similar words in the mouth of Moses (Deuteronomy 32) and Jeremiah (Jeremiah 5). Jesus laments over God's chosen but faithless people.

But Jesus' sorrow does not turn him away from the people; he is prepared to walk into suffering, using his authority to liberate others from suffering. There is no sense in which Jesus seeks to control or castigate either the father or his son in their weakness. The emphasis is entirely on Jesus' word calling from deep to deep. His question to the father draws him even further into human helplessness. Jesus gives his heart to listening, and it is from there, in a costly challenge to despair that's so unexpected, so fresh, so powerful, that he finds the challenge which provokes faith, '"If *you* can?" All things are possible to him who believes.'

Jesus' word is also liberating for the son. He speaks sternly, not to the boy, but to the spirit who is holding him prisoner. And he acts quickly to avoid a spectacle being made of the boy.

> *And when Jesus saw that a crowd came running together, he rebuked the unclean spirit, saying to it, 'You dumb and deaf spirit, I command you, come out of him, and never enter him again.' After crying out and convulsing him terribly, it came out.*

Jesus' word is addressed to the root cause of the symptoms, and by this word this spirit is evicted from its unnatural home for ever. The inhuman 'it' of the spirit is cleaved from the human 'him' of the boy, leaving Jesus to gather up the fragments of his human being:

> *And the boy was like a corpse; so that most of them said, 'He is dead.' But Jesus took him by the hand and lifted him up, and he arose.*

The language of the RSV lingers on the loving action of Christ. The divine power that raises the vulnerable is the pull of a human hand. And what this hand does is set the boy on his feet. It is a costly act: the spirit only leaves after crying out and convulsing the boy terribly. But it is also a simple human act that restores the boy from being like a corpse to the stature of a person.

Jesus' awareness of his mission takes him, with all the power of God at his command, into the heart of spiritual conflict. And there he becomes vulnerable. More than once Mark makes the point that Christ reaches out in tenderness to the people he heals. Jesus lifts up Simon's mother-in-law who has a fever, and later the ruler's dead daughter, with the beautiful words 'Talitha cumi', which means, 'Little girl, I say to you, arise'. He becomes an instrument totally dedicated to speaking God's healing word. He opens himself to the suffering and frailty of his fellow human beings, and to the power of God to save. This lesson is spelled out at the end of the story:

And when he had entered the house, his disciples asked him privately, 'Why could we not cast it out?' And he said to them, 'This kind cannot be driven out by anything but prayer [other ancient authorities add *and fasting*].'

Actually Jesus *has not* prayed in the story, unless we call his words to the boy a 'prayer of command' (Francis McNutt) or 'authoritative prayer' (Richard Foster). Here Jesus speaks for God rather than in intercession to God. This man carries the authority and power of someone who lives in absolute dependence on God, whose power is God's own power. Earlier in the gospel Mark tells another story which shows this. A woman who suffered from haemorrhages for twelve years was healed when she touched his cloak. She had come up behind Jesus out of the crowd in the hope of remaining unnoticed; but, Mark says, Jesus was at once aware that power had gone out of him (5.30). The power Jesus carries in his person is as mysterious and untameable as the God he represents.

For Mark prayer is the way Jesus in solitude opens his whole self to the dark mystery of God. The power he gains from prayer cannot be used for his own ends: it leads him on in mission; it renders him available to the sick and sinful; it propels him into battle with the powers of evil. The climax of this way of prayer comes from the cross. Jesus cries out, 'My God, my God, why hast thou forsaken me?' reaching out into the darkness for a God whose power and presence has been known, maybe right until that terrible moment. And still Jesus cannot do anything other than reach out to a hidden God. Prayer was his way of living; now it is his way of dying.[3]

The Power of a Prayerful Life

The story Mark tells is a battle in which two spiritual forces for good meet to crush the power of evil: the vulnerability expressed in the father's cry and the power expressed in Jesus' command which meets it. Earlier on, using the father's plea as an example of faith, we spent time looking at prayer as a cry from the heart; now, using Jesus' life as an example of faith, let us set prayer in the wider context of living for God as an instrument of his will.

The idea of being an instrument of God's will is prone to misunderstanding. My experience is that Christians suspect that God's mind is made up on most things; our job is to do his bidding. The story we have read tells us just the opposite. God-in-Christ goes to extreme lengths to unearth the desires of our hearts, so that he can act on them. Prayer isn't there to tow our hearts into line with fate; it is there so that in the midst of our feelings of powerlessness we might find freedom for ourselves and our world. Jesus'

---

3 The marginal addition to the final verse of 'and fasting' bears out the sense of prayer being a sign of total dependence on God. In Jewish spirituality, fasting was seen as an aid to prayer. It was a discipline used by the children of God to remind them of their dependence on God, above even eating.

prayer in the Garden of Gethsemane is sometimes taken as definite evidence that prayer is about learning to bow to God's will by suppressing our own desires. But once again Mark has different lesson of faith to tell. In the garden Jesus throws himself upon God's mercy and his loving purposes for the world, leaving the question open of whether his Father can find a way to remove the cup of suffering from him. His submission to whatever God's will may be *once he has been heard in prayer* frees him to face betrayal and abandonment, because he can trust God to do what is good. Meanwhile, his disciples who sleep rather than pray fail to follow him into danger.

Those who pray, then, need not fear that they will be required to abandon hope. Quite the contrary; Charles Eliot in his book *Praying the Kingdom* wrote that prayer can change events:

> If we see prayer as a means of releasing God's power into the world, of enabling him to pour his transforming love into the critical centres of decision-making and activity, we begin to see paradoxically that we are not powerless at all. Our power to transform the world is God's power. That is hard to comprehend. Like so many spiritual truths, it is so simple that it takes some grasping. Certainly the mainline churches have forgotten it or are afraid of it. I was asked to address the Synod of the Church of England on world development at the time of the publication of the Brandt Report. I concluded an analysis of the Report by saying that in my view, the proper response of the Church was one of, quite literally, prayer and fasting. Four days later I received an angry, stinging rebuke from a senior church official. 'I was very disappointed', he wrote, 'that all you could suggest was prayer. The last thing we want is to return to is that kind of pietism…' When I enquired what help a major church-based charity gave its supporters to pray for the poor and the vulnerable, the answer was revealing: 'Oh God, we don't want people to think that all they've got to do is pray.'

It is faithless to expect too little, even when we are vulnerable and can see no way that God can bring deliverance. We defend ourselves from being further hurt and disappointed by not hoping for too much. The way forward, though, is not to put our trust in the results our power can achieve, but to trust in Jesus to let our power be exercised in vulnerability so that it mirrors his, whatever the results.

It is a paradox that, in our society, where more disease than ever is treatable, we are more than ever aware of what lies outside our power. AIDS frightens us, not just because it is a fatal condition for those who contract it, but because something has arrived in our civilised and sophisticated world uninvited and is getting the better of us, despite all that we spend to conquer it. It threatens our fantasy of human power and progress. Mark's story of the healing of the epileptic demoniac has a happy ending. But we have to realise that even epilepsy caused by deep and malicious forces may well be easier to cure than conditions like AIDS, dementia or chronic schizophrenia. In these cases we do have power to bring deliverance from all that dehumanises and oppresses persons, but not power to 'make people better'.

As I said earlier, it is easy to overlook or disown the power we have as Christians. Never more so than when we come up against dead-end situations, when all that we can hope is that things do not get worse too quickly. Take for instance the heartache and burden of an elderly relative with dementia. Medicine can offer no cure; never again will she be the person she was. She may eventually not even recognise her husband or children. How can we talk here of power? My answer is that we can—of a power that expresses itself in vulnerability, and so which brings deliverance to the one society labels victim.

Let me expand on this. Medicine offers many fine techniques for the healing of bodies, which can be used with compassion and love. I would not for a moment want to detract from that. But the dark side of society's emphasis on healing is seen in the lack of resources and respect given to those who cannot be successes in these terms. They are the ones who can become outcast. Mark's story has something to say to this, as it is not just about a healing; it tells of a deliverance from an evil power, which is a sign of resurrection. The boy who is raised is transformed from being a passive outcast possessed by a spirit, to a lifeless 'corpse', to a person.

Followers of Jesus have the power, through faith, to enter into 'hopeless' situations and so transform them. We have authority to use our gifts, skills and graces in the service of others. Christians need not be afraid of the spirits that make people outcast, because their authority does not come from others but from God. In those cases where no possibility for healing is foreseeable it is tempting to lose faith in God and imagine our only power to be to contain the problem. Containment is important—to deaden confusion, prevent self-injury and relieve pain, and so on—but Christians can't be content with this. Resurrection healing in Mark's story turns a boy from a corpse into a being a person. It puts the 'he' back into his body.

A lesson of faith from Mark is that those who pray can, like Christ, become agents of resurrection. They have the power to confer personhood on those whom society fears and calls victim. This power is not the same as that offered by medical technique. It cannot be aimed at a particular outcome. Rather, it is a superhuman power for good that stands against all that is evil and dehumanising. We experience it as the courage to step out from behind our defences, to give ourselves in vulnerability to the corpses, even if we are wounded by our own or others' human frailty in the process. A nun once sent me this poem:

'Vulnerability
        that quality in a man that enables him to be defenceless
        unfettered by ties of fear
        unchained by ideologies
        lacking the will to impose or manipulate

        gate-less, wall-less, reachable,
        unlocked, unblocked,
        open-armed, growing,
        in constant process of definition.
        wanton
        foolishly exposed to life
            and its crashing impact,
        free.'

One way of reaching out, literally, is by touch. Touch allows us to use the power we have in a Christ-like way, to make ourselves vulnerable to others. Outside a hospice or hospital, often the only socially accepted means of touch is a handshake, but even a handshake is a way in which we put ourselves in another's grasp. However it is offered, touch can be an extremely important way to promote the meeting of persons. We risk contact; we choose contact with this one particular person; we feel flesh like ours; we offer ourselves in the flesh. Touch is a vehicle by which our lives are bound together in partnership and openness.[4]

Praying, too, is a way of reaching out because it is the way in which we exchange our hopelessness about what cannot change for trust in God and faith in God's future. This is a process that begins with our learning to identify with the vulnerable. The cry 'I believe; help my unbelief!' is not spoken by an individual for his own benefit but by a father who carries the burden of care for his whole family. Prayer does not work by pretending that we see solutions to intractable suffering and weakness but by carrying the pain we have learnt to share into the mystery of God and giving it away to him. Faith is our refusal to let the prison bars of the cell of suffering block the prospect of the dawn.

In touching and praying we are not creating temporary illusions of care to make us feel better, ones which have no real effect. Our acts of self-giving beyond technique are theological acts; we make them in faith. With

---

4   See chapter 3 in my book *Stronger than Death* (DLT, London 1993) for an exploration of how touch, silence and speech can form a language of service.

'unconditional receptiveness' to the action of God we confer on society's corpses the power of resurrection. Faith won't offer escape from a sense of helplessness, because faith in the resurrection means giving up knowing how things are bound to turn out. No one but God knows how resurrection will be applied to life. Jesus himself, even though he predicted that he would rise again after three days, still experienced dereliction on the cross. He had no neat way of bringing God's future into his darkness. The present had to be suffered through and joined to the future by a cry of despair.

The story of the healing of the epileptic demoniac gives us one, particular example of resurrection power at work, but it doesn't close off other outcomes. The gospel remains open to the future, as the abrupt ending of Mark's suggests:

> *And they went out and fled from the tomb; for trembling and astonishment had come upon them; and they said nothing to any one, for they were afraid.*

What resurrection does is strike fear into the hearts of the women who visited the tomb. Like them, we cannot fathom the power of resurrection; but we know that if a corpse is what a person has become, that is not how it will remain, the future is open to God.

A story that helps me to see this started with a telephone call. Did I know that Eve, a student member of my congregation, had been suddenly taken ill? An internal rupture and an emergency operation had taken her to death's door and back in two days. When I visited she was sitting up in bed, cheerful and joking. Two months later, the shock caught up with her. She had fainted when out with her friends and had had other panic attacks. Eve was further troubled because she thought she should simply be grateful to be alive. But now she remembered a nurse crying over her bedside and, later, an emotional consultant telling Eve that she would never get that close to dying again. The vulnerability shown by these two people had broken into her depths. Their love brought disquiet to Eve's heart, but in the disruption and darkness were the seeds of resurrection.

The abrupt end to Mark's Gospel points both backwards and forwards; forwards to this dark, mysterious reality being in our midst and backwards to the stories which interpret it to us. So, in light of these gospel stories we are freed to wonder, to fantasise about how things might turn out in God's power.

The Christian 'fantasy' of resurrection is far stronger than the other fantasies we live by: *political* fantasies of a classless society or of efficient government, and *psychological* ideas—achieving mental equilibrium or overcoming trauma. All these enduring fantasies, myths, stories—call them what you will—bring hope that things can change. But we should cling above all other fantasies to resurrection, because it is more than an idea or an ideal. It has already been realised by Jesus in his life, death and resurrection.

We believe in an awesome story of transformation, which is real but incomplete. We must be grasped by it and let it empower how we care for others. We must not let ourselves be tied down by the limits of human hope in the power of technique, and equally we must not let ourselves be suffocated by demands of society to make people normal, cheaply.

Julian of Norwich, whose parable we read earlier, was a woman of great Christian optimism. She didn't overlook the pain of the human condition; in fact, the place where she looked for hope was in the heart of suffering, in the face of the crucified Lord. In the words with which I finish she wrestles with the paradox of the reality of sin and judgement on the one hand and the reality of universal love of God on the other. She is led to a confident affirmation of resurrection-power, a power which reaches down into human faithlessness and hopelessness in the suffering humanity of Jesus Christ:

'In my folly before this time I often wondered why, through the great prescient wisdom of God, the beginning of sin was not prevented. For then it seemed to me that all would have been well...But Jesus...said: Sin is necessary, but all will be well, and all will be well, and every kind of thing will be well. In this naked word 'sin', our Lord brought generally to mind all which is not good, and the shameful contempt and the direst tribulation which he endured for us in this life, and his death and all his pains, and the passions, spiritual and bodily, of all his creatures.'